My Aunt's Abortion

My Aunt's Abortion

Jane Rosenberg LaForge

BLAZEVOX[BOOKS]
Buffalo, New York

My Aunt's Abortion
by Jane Rosenberg LaForge

Published by BlazeVOX [books]

Printed in the United States of America

Interior design and typesetting by Geoffrey Gatza

First Edition
ISBN: 978-1-60964-417-8
Library of Congress Control Number: 2022942733

BlazeVOX [books]
131 Euclid Ave
Kenmore, NY 14217
Editor@blazevox.org

publisher of weird little books

BlazeVOX [books]

blazevox.org

21 20 19 18 17 16 15 14 13 12 01 02 03 04 05 06 07 08 09 10 11

BlazeVOX

Acknowledgments

The following works were previously published or are scheduled to appear in these journals:

Narrative Reproduction: *The Smart Set*

Statistics: *Writing in a Woman's Voice*

The Water Method Women: *The Blue Nib*

How My Aunt's Abortion Was Like a Fern: *Pomona Valley Review*

Weeds: *Spotlong Review*

1967 or Approximate: *Silkworm*

Scenes From My Parents' Marriage: *The Awakenings Review*

The Set Dresser: *Loch Raven Review*

The After Plants: *Pirene's Fountain*

Reception: *Pirene's Fountain*

My Father Attempts to Explain Billie Holiday to Us: *The Chiron Review*

The Remains: *The Blue Nib*

The Lost: *The Awakenings Review*

After the Abortion: Construction: *The Awakenings Review*

After the Abortion: The Cuttings: *The Awakenings Review*

Time Is Relative: *The Mark Literary Review*

Triangles: *Sledgehammer Lit*

From the Gutter: *Writing in a Woman's Voice*

Largess: *Schuylkill Valley Journal*

After the Abortion III: *The Awakenings Review*

Table of Contents

My Aunt's Abortion

This book is dedicated to my cousin, Dona Tao.

Narrative Reproduction

Once upon a time, there was an alligator who wanted to be a purse. He got his wish, but he was still hungry. He opened his mouth and the department store worker stuffed tissue in his mouth. This was a story I wrote, and my now late aunt borrowed, for a class she was taking at college. She was supposed to write a fable, something like one of Aesop's fables or Kipling's Just So stories, but she couldn't think of anything. My mother suggested she use my tale of the alligator, from one of my eighth-grade homework assignments. It was 1975, and my aunt had seemingly recovered from an illegal abortion that had almost killed her a few years earlier.

My aunt was going to college to become a special education teacher. She wanted to work with learning disabled and developmentally delayed children, and was majoring in psychology. She never became a teacher, as was the case with all of her plans. Something always went astray, whether it was her education, her career, her personal life, or her retirement. My family blamed her frustrations on some deeply-seated trait, like a bad attitude. What other explanation could there be, since all the rest of us had been able to secure some modicum of happiness, through hard work, diligence, our vaunted educations. I wonder if the answer lies in the circumstances she was dealt, consequences she could not have anticipated. Perhaps she should have anticipated them. Does that mean she deserved them?

These are the questions I've been asking myself over the past decade, just as Republicans initiated their campaign to recriminalize abortion. In 2013 South Dakota became the first state to pass a "heartbeat" bill, prohibiting abortions if a fetal heartbeat is detected within the uterus. The U.S. Supreme Court threw out South Dakota's law, and attempts by at least ten other states to severely curtail abortion rights in the same manner were also overruled by the courts. But that was before the newly emboldened conservative majority of the nation's highest court overturned nearly a half-century of legal precedent in 2022. The landmark Roe v. Wade decision was egregiously wrong from the start, the court said.

With abortion no longer a constitutional right, the decision in Dobbs v. Jackson (Mississippi) Women's Health Association, No. 19-1392, leaves state legislators with the power to decide if, when, and how abortion is available within their jurisdiction. In the weeks between the leak of a draft decision on May 2 and the handing down of the final decision on June 24, 2022, commentators, activists, and experts predicted that as many as 26 states would automatically ban abortion through the use of so-called "trigger laws." Mary Ziegler, a legal historian at Florida State University College of Law, took note of these potential bans being considered and risked a prediction. "…at least for a time after Roe is decimated," she wrote in *The New York Times,* "there could be not two Americas when it comes to abortion, but three: one in which almost any abortion is a crime, one in which abortion is broadly available and one in which abortion is heavily restricted but not altogether available."

That last possibility mirrors the situation my aunt faced, when abortion was legal in California, but legal abortion was inaccessible. It was a familiar scenario even in the world Roe v. Wade made; a 2019 article in *The New York Times* estimated 11 million American women lived in counties without abortion clinics, because state regulations and other factors effectively outlawed a facet of women's health care that was supposed to be protected.

My aunt's abortion occurred sometime in the late 1960's, before Roe but sometime after the state Legislature and then governor, Ronald Reagan, made abortion legal in a limited number of cases. Under the 1967 Therapeutic Abortion Law, a committee of medical professionals had to approve the procedure as necessary for the patient's health before each abortion could be performed. That committee sometimes included a district attorney, to ensure that any claims of rape or incest were real. An estimated 100,000 illegal abortions were being performed in the state annually before the law's passage, according to a remembrance of the legislation published in 2013 in *Real Clear Politics*. This didn't include abortions performed in Tijuana, where women "were taking their lives in their hands," according to state Supreme Court records. Stopping these "criminal" abortions, as a landmark state Supreme Court case termed them, was one of the primary motivations behind passage of the 1967 law. "Induced illegal abortion" was "one of the most important causes" of "infertility and disease," according to a 1966 study cited in the Supreme Court decision.

But once therapeutic abortion became law, people continued to seek the procedure clandestinely, because so few met the law's standards. For instance, only 600 legal abortions were performed in California in 1967, according to an archive of state abortion statistics. Meanwhile, Patricia Maginnis, known for creating the first list of clandestine abortion providers in the country, continued giving her classes on how to perform a self-abortion, according to a 2018 profile of Maginnis in *Slate*. The original state law, from 1850, still proscribed a five-year prison sentence for women who "submit or solicit" an abortion. That law wasn't overturned until 1969, when the state Supreme Court called the the state's statutory tangle of laws "an invalid abridgment of women's rights," effectively making abortion legal in California.

My aunt was in her late twenties, drifting and heartsick over the death of her father, whom she adored, when she likely got pregnant. She was living with her mother, and had already been married and divorced. When she worked, it was as a secretary or a "Kelly Girl," with the Russell Kelly Office Service. Her mother complained to me and my father that my aunt often dashed out of the apartment after having nothing more for breakfast than a glass of milk with the era's equivalent of protein powder, then known as Carnation's Instant Breakfast.

This was not the future anybody had envisioned for my aunt; she was the "good times baby." Before she was born, my father recalled, the family frequently couldn't "make" the rent, so they moved. They moved often, sometimes in the middle of the night. By the time my aunt was born, though, a booming, pre-World War II economy had lifted the household up and out of its doldrums, and into better apartments with long-term leases. My aunt went to summer camp; I found her letters home. Her Sweet Sixteen party was held in Las Vegas. A friend remembers seeing my aunt pull into the driveway of the family home sometime after she graduated from high school. She was driving a convertible, and wearing a fur coat.

I remember her being pregnant, with an extended belly. At the time she told me not to squeeze her too hard because she had a hernia. What I didn't know was that she had gone to my parents about the pregnancy, and my father had offered to adopt the baby once it was born. My mother agreed, but not to my father's conditions: that the baby could never know who its real parents were. My mother said this was impossible, as my sister and I were old enough to know where babies came from, and that this new sibling obviously wouldn't have come to us in the regular way. For about a week, after I had gone to bed, I heard my parents arguing, although I didn't know what it was about. The actual words did not travel past their locked bedroom door. But the anger and frustration, the volume of their fights, seeped into my room, on the other side of the wall.

My mother said my aunt took matters into her own hands, and got an abortion. Based on what I know about family history, I'd say this was between between 1966 and 1969. The abortion was somehow botched, however, and she carried the fetus to term. It was stillborn, which must have been a relief to my parents, and possibly to my aunt. I don't know, because this is my mother's versions of events. She told me this only long after she divorced my father, as she spilled a bunch of family secrets, to convince me that I could recover from my own failures, whatever they might be. My mother never said a critical word about my aunt over this business, yet she remained incensed that my father had been unreasonable during this episode. It haunted their marriage for years afterward.

My father told another story after my mother died. He said my aunt asked for money for an abortion. He gave it to her, during a secret meeting on a cliff road outside our neighborhood. A neighbor saw my father with a much younger, attractive woman, and told my mother. My father said he was able to talk my mother down from this gossip, although given what happened later in their life together, this too likely amounted to another cut against their marriage. My aunt, meanwhile, still had to get the abortion. He said she went to an "animal doctor," but I acknowledge that my father was not the most reliable narrator of family history. I don't know whether he was being derisive or figurative.

One morning, my grandmother called my father from the hospital to say my aunt had a kidney infection. Or that is what he told us, me and my sister. This must have been the genesis of peritonitis, an inflammation of the abdominal lining that affected her lungs, an illness that never seemed to end. Peritonitis is sometimes caused by cirrhosis of the liver, but that wasn't likely in my aunt's case. She rarely drank to excess, and was never diagnosed with a liver problem. That she became ill long after, it seemed to me, the botched pregnancy; and that my father's version of events was so different than my mother's, could mean that my aunt had not one, but two illegal abortions. I realize all this in retrospect, as I try to put all these disparate accounts together.

However—and wherever--my aunt obtained her abortion or abortions, the safest, now widely used method, vacuum aspiration with a Karman cannula, had yet to be invented. The *Los Angeles Times* obituary for the cannula's inventor—a psychologist who served a two-and-a-half-year state prison sentence in the 1950's for performing an abortion in which the woman died--places its invention in the early 1970s and its first demonstration in 1972. Current medical literature discusses the possibility of sepsis after abortion, but not peritonitis. Yet peritonitis caused by abortion was "of the greatest interest in Finland," according to a 1950 article in a Scandinavian medical journal on how to treat the infection.

By 1970, my aunt's peritonitis had affected her lungs. I know this because I watched her undergo respiratory therapy in the apartment she shared with my grandmother. She had to use a nebulizer and do exercises. One called for my aunt to rest on a slanted board upside down, and beat at her lung cavities with her hands. My grandmother was constantly washing the nebulizer equipment, in soap and scalding water. I remember the pride she took in completing this task, as though there was finally some way she could be useful. The equipment had to be perfectly sterile, she said, because my aunt's immune system was "like a baby's."

I can place this routine so well because it was during the time I was frequently shipped out of the house; my mother had what was then called a "nervous breakdown" that year, and was institutionalized for several months. Aside from my aunt's abortion, several other domestic disasters had befallen us, and finally they threw my mother into a cycle of manias she could not come back from. Once released from the hospital, she was profoundly depressed, seemingly dedicated only to her cigarettes, coffee, and somnambulance. At least this is how my father saw it, but there was a lot more to her recovery. From what I witnessed, it was tedious and difficult. By her telling, it was inevitable. The retreat of her hormones, or menopause, did the trick, she told me. I also think divorcing my father helped, but again, that is another story of consequences, intended and otherwise.

I don't blame my aunt, or her abortion, for my mother's nervous breakdown. I don't blame her for all that happened afterward. My father's unreasonable demand about the potential adoption likely had more to do with the implosion of my family than anything my aunt did. Suddenly, as my mother was maneuvering through a slew of conflicts, she discovered she had to do so alone, because her husband was undependable, in his own peculiar, pig-headed way. I'll allow that my aunt's abortion became the disaster that it was because of the circumstances of my family, uniquely unqualified to deal with troubles. But the story of her abortion is about what happens when the most private matters are forced into a public realm, where the details can be debated, become a source of resentment, and ultimately infect the merely peripherally-involved in the procedure. What we might not yet understand is how the consequences of illegal abortion extend beyond the person who may or may not survive the procedure. But if my family's experience is any indicator, we might soon find out how vast and pernicious the lack of real abortion options is.

I can't put an exact date on my aunt's recovery. Sometime in the early '70s, she was well enough to attend the annual 4th of July party my parents' best friends gave each year. Their daughter was scandalized, slightly, when she walked in on my aunt and a young law student, making out in the bathroom. They were fully clothed and probably no further than first base, and the daughter has admitted to me over the years that she'd always been taken aback by the kind of woman my aunt was. At the height of the women's movement, our mothers were still housewives. Their uniforms consisted of jeans, blouses and sports shirts, Keds sneakers; their regimens seemed governed by cigarettes, coffee, housework and carpooling. My aunt was the first woman we children knew to be glamorous. She wore jewelry, a gold necklace I remember, with a cloisonné locket. I never saw what was inside that locket. I watched her powder her nose from a compact; she was the only woman we knew who wore makeup. She dressed in silk blouses and fancy slacks. She wore high heels. She occasionally passed down some of her wardrobe to me, though the clothes never looked as good on me as they did on her.

My aunt also moved to her own apartment around this time, and enrolled in junior college. She later transferred to a state university, but ran into trouble with finishing her degree. A friend got her a job as a "building engineer," or janitor, which she worked nights. My aunt and mother remained friends: they played pranks and backed each other in marathon political arguments with my father. While I was in high school, as my mother explained how birth control pills worked, my aunt showed me hers. They were prescribed to alleviate pain from ovarian cysts, she said. She would have been in her early forties by then, and I remember her dating occasionally. But she never remarried, or found a partner serious enough to tell us about.

I was always excited when my aunt came over. She didn't bring gifts, but she always had some adventure to tell, like the time she went to a Hollywood party. But it was not a real Hollywood party, she said; it was someone's idea of a Hollywood party. A hollow Hollywood party, with all the sex and drugs, but no celebrities. When they weren't fighting over politics, my father and my aunt spoke openly, even whimsically, about the travails of their extended, immigrant family: money problems, life-changing illnesses, petty jealousies, divorce and domestic abuse, even mild vendettas. But the abortions never made it to these dinner table discussions.

In 1981 my parents divorced, sundering the link between my aunt and my mother. My mother remembered her sister-in-law as "fun." When my father underwent heart bypass surgery, my aunt volunteered to prepare his meals, but they argued over whether he should pay her once he was on his feet. They argued over money a lot, especially five years after my father's heart surgery, when their mother died. I cleaned out my father's apartment some seventeen years after that, once he was moved to assisted living. I found all the documents, including the letter my aunt wrote, demanding my father pay her more than $100,000. She had carefully calculated the sum, based on the one-time worth of the then-defunct family business. But there was nothing left. My grandmother had lived on it, and then my father went into debt. I was supporting him by then.

Some cousins were upset by her behavior after my grandmother died. "This is how she mourned her mother," one cousin said bitterly: with a textbook and a highlighter so she could keep studying. She was always taking a class. Later she appeared at my father's apartment, where my grandmother had lived, and confiscated what she believed to be hers. The rap against my aunt, as some relatives put it, was that she was negative, spoiled and self-centered; that she didn't think she had to work like everybody else, because she was better than everyone else. Once, she said, her parents told her she couldn't be friends with someone from school, because the girl's family did not have as much money as her family did. "And you know something?" she told me. "They were right."

"I'm sorry her life was not so happy," another cousin wrote to me after my aunt's death, about four years ago. As I've tried to piece my aunt's life together, and whether her illegal abortion(s) contributed to her unhappiness, I've had to confront the good and the bad about my aunt, who must have always felt uncomfortable in her skin, given her circumstances. My mother recalled that on the day her parents were to meet my father's family, her future in-laws were late because they were arguing over what my aunt, then nineteen, should wear to the dinner date. My aunt tried to become a model in New York; one photograph from her portfolio is all that I can salvage from that effort. Sometime during the 1960s, she tried becoming an artist; the center of her bedroom at my grandmother's apartment was a charcoal drawing she worked on, seemingly forever. Eventually it was framed and hung on the wall, but I had to ask her what the small black and white square in the middle of the picture depicted. It was a man and woman embracing.

When my grandmother was living with my father in her late 80s or early 90s—we never knew how old she was—my aunt said my grandmother beat her as a child. I found this hard to believe since my grandmother had loved me as only a grandmother could. My father had said many times over what an extrordinary mother she had been to him as a child, how hard she worked to shepherd him through a difficult childhood. My aunt was nuts, my father said; others said she was delusional. She "kind of lost her mind after the peritonitis," another cousin told me. She died at age 78 of heart arrhythmia, largely because she wouldn't treat it. She didn't believe she had the money to do so.

When I think about my aunt, I wonder whether her story will become the stuff of vintage documentaries: the kind where the filmmaker looks back at a seemingly unbelievable era in our nation's history, when we didn't understand what we take for granted now. A long time ago, this was a country where women could rarely decide their own fate. If any woman dare challenge this system, take the course of her life into her own hands, the course of her own body, they would suffer in a myriad of ways. I use this cliché of "myriad" because we are always finding new ways to punish women in our society; the ingredients of shame, loss of privacy, and control over the body, are always the same, but the various bureaucracies and intrusive moves and regulations seem to multiply, if not mutate. Now my aunt is one of those fables that grow out of these cycles, and fables are open to interpretation. You have the freedom to choose yours.

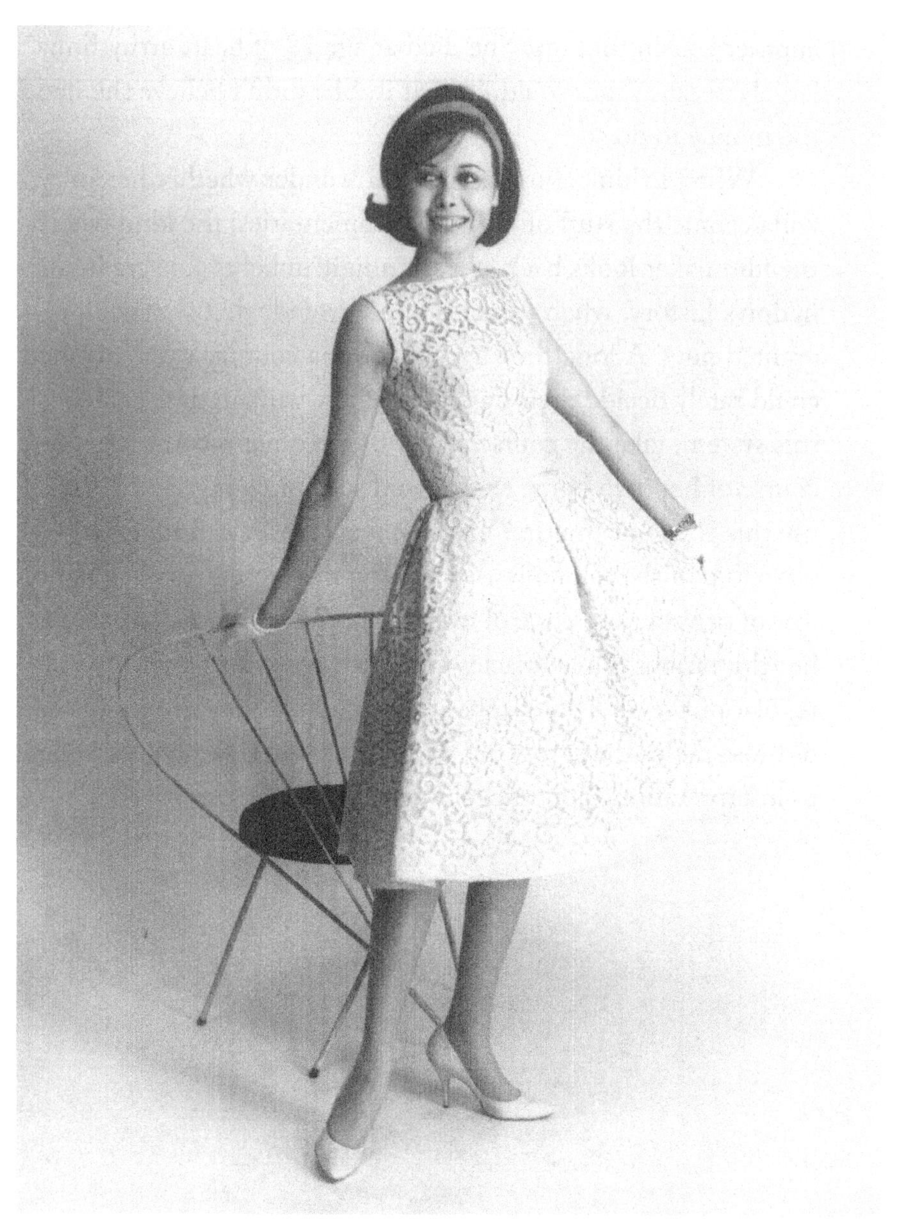

Modeling Portfolio, date unknown

Disclosure

Of course this could all be fanciful,
what I've pieced together from vestiges
or trace amounts, without the substance
to build a body out of, but outtakes,
unguarded moments when parents believe
their offspring are incapable or non-comprehending.
Wherever the source, we think we know
the setting, hot and claustrophobic,
drinking blood or bleating with disease,
disputed real estate that is both zero
point and epicenter, held in plain
contempt because familiarity breeds
exclusively in the female and contains
multitudes, potentially. Unlike the lining
of an oyster, the grand prospects inherent
in arc and prism, the shape of the nurturer
is as precious as the outcome—no wonder
my mother loved pearls. A sliding scale
of quicksilver, readily tallied, even
through her callouses. When it comes
to eggs and chickens, scientists say it's best
to think not of the creature first equipped
to make that egg, but how advanced it
must have been, evolutionarily speaking,
to shelter that kind of vulnerability
at the expense of its own preservation.
They say nothing about progeny
that get in the way of the wolves
their parents become, a metamorphosis
heretofore unconsidered, yet alive
again, under our rekindled art
of the possible.

Statistics

Courtesy of the institute
that wouldn't take my call

about the one dead woman
from a procedure half a century

earlier because she was an aunt
to no one. History registers only

in terabytes, in epiphanies
and readily identifiable wallops,

how the number of women seeking
to end pregnancies was small,

even manageable, so long as it
was only for the life of the mother.

This is what my mother meant
when she cried out, "Don't be

a statistic, Janey," because
studies show it is better

to break a surface directly,
rather than to poke blindly;

a push is more organic
than a vacuum or a pump;

a pile of dead skin is preferable
to a pitted face, or uterus.

Now, on to the scars.

The Water Method Women

1.

My grandmother loved the ocean.
She said its air helped her asthma.
She drank a brand of ginger ale
that burned my throat on its way
down, on top of the tea without
sugar. This must be what happens
when you grow up landlocked,
White Russia as far as the eyes
might track as you play with your
rag dolls on the roof, the only
memory that survived the transit.
This is what you must teach your
grandchildren; that wheat does
not feed the starving and it
ripens like something female,
ever on the verge of stinging,
or curdling into an afterlife
of infection and soreness.
Before she married my grandfather,
she supposedly ran away from Los Angeles
to San Francisco for someone
else, draw into her lungs what
the climate made tactile,
a woolen restorative in its
finest, most delicate color.
Then she came back, though
we don't know the whole of
that story, only the struggle
subsequent to escape the bedrock
and inhale where breath could
be with salt and moisture braided.

2.

Her daughter chose the deserts
on the other side of the hill,
the water channeled through
cement to the harbor, an
unnatural opening that had to
be combed through regularly
by equipment and engineers.
Otherwise the liquid progressed
to vinegar, the final stage
unless you're counting
disappearance. My parents
discovered quite by accident
how vinegar in salad dressing,
left open on the table,
deterred bees from circling
over the meat. So we always
had some extra, as if a dish
of tears, for our outdoor meals.
Both sides of the family went
after the war and politics
like a second Pacific theater.
I watched her sweat as though
drowning in her failed pregnancies.
She drank instant coffee,
served in the mug my parents
found so hilarious: MADE IN
JAPAN on one side,
the rising sun on the other.
Her brother always said
we should be upfront with
our intentions and origins,
ultimately risky
and foreign.

The Night My Aunt Got Pregnant

But it was only a premonition
of her death,
or a picture, flat
and two dimensional, instead of
the real thing, an unspeakable act,
an experiment or a test, perhaps:
in a moment of weakness, a break
in the dirge, a sowing of dregs,
a one-in-a-million convergence
of flash and liquid,
idle hands and too much evidence.
But in that vision, you might find
a shadow, like resemblance,
her life spent *in extremis,*
before rot and compromise secured
their ramparts although
that is a natural process,
underway long before
compulsory instinct
gives out, and the body,
still young, believes
in its own definitions
of past and present.

Mulholland Drive

You learn to set scenes within a beveled
square, a stage and curtains like the bottom
edge of a lip, or a convex screen across
a flattened dimension; or sometimes improvised
out of a car window, the passenger side
or the front windshield, a fish-eyed

vision that holds the city as if the road
were singing a lullaby or a prayer.
The Irish one, about the wind at your back,
or the road becomes a crown unraveled,
as if the curvature of a sphere beaten into

the flats, the audience, beneath and below
the auteur. The answer belongs to the interpreters,
the gossips, when they hear of a young woman
made up like Audrey Heburn, hair wrapped in a scarf
as if for her role opposite Albert Finney
and a sports car; but her co-star is a married man,

nervous in his dry-cleaned shirt, the type
narcs sport without ever having gotten a
a memo on the uniform. His wife collects
them each week in a bundle. The bag man
in the exchange of intentions and business.
This was all before I had read about the architecture

of synagogues: the lobby as a prelude to
the sanctuary; the sanctuary as prelude to the ark;
the ten commandments waiting as if a body,
maybe a dictator's, maybe a saint's, maybe
something ruined by a communion that saves
the believers, and for the others, poisons

arteries, whole boulevards, lungs as if
distinguished by neon pathways, routes
that ants create as they burrow through
sand in a cross section of plastic, like they're
playing on TV, a toy someone always brings
to your birthday party, but your mother
can't stand it, and sends it away. Not in

her house, carved into rock that was
once a hilltop; designed by a family friend
out of spite, bought and paid for by various
relatives. Cleared of all tragedy, and therefore
all catharsis. No one can find what you don't
let out or broadcast, unless they're driving by
before the director makes his cut.

Analgesic

If we could communicate through powders:
moon dust or pounded gravel—
what would be the conclusions?
That silence owns the greatest
hunger to be heard;
the desires of an absence
are the least amenable
to being fulfilled;
that tissue in the mouth,
in the pouch no more substantial
than a puff of air, a swelling
of abdomen: that is the most
difficult to bear, to ease
with an application of cold.
When you put a pin
in a balloon, it might not necessarily
pop as science demands,
but twist and suffer,
trying to hold onto the life
that was never yours
to command.

My Aunt's Abortion

1.

I don't know whether the lights hummed
like at the dentist's, or if there were lights
or a single bulb over a wobbly table;
I don't know whether there was a table,
or an analgesic or a nerve blocker.

But there was a body; nothing happens
without a body, prone, possibly on a blanket
though not likely. Perhaps on the floor,
the lowest point since every room has one,
every building, a zero level, bottom, soil.

I think it might have been like the seed
struggling as a trapeze artist would
after a bad launch, the suspense
and adrenaline regardless
of outcome. I witnessed as much as
the roots of a plant sought purchase
in a plastic petri dish I was given,
with a transparent culture; the seed
already open like the roly-poly
bugs that crawled in our father's garden
when they felt unthreatened, before
we kids got to them.

How we abused those bugs,
kicking and flinging them over the fence,
as they curled themselves into taut little shields
of exoskeleton. There was too much
we didn't understand back then:
how those insects are useful,
clearing away decomposition;
or how money worked, where cousins

came from, our grandfather's will,
who got what, although it added up
all to nothing.

2.

I assume she hemorrhaged in pulses,
the heart pushing out what
the serration could not catch,
what was in the womb
but as shadow,
not as prediction
but as past, proof
of future concepts
like a body that is neither infant nor child
but as a pool of tendencies
and events, what marks a pattern
though patterns refer only to what
we perceive, and not to what actually
might exist. A daydream, then,
of cousins and lineage,
what it means to prosper
in what once was
a hostile environment.
This bleeding was the end
of that fantasy, and as the fluids
were expelled, they sought
to drown
an entire family.

3.

When no one sees the scar,
a change in structure
and surface tension,
it is still there, bright
in the darkness. An exclamation
point, instructions on a pirated

map, the cartoon lexicon
for exertion when a character
takes off: Bugs Bunny on
the run from Elmer Fudd,
Wiley E. Coyote chasing after
his own rocket once he discovers
his missteps. We laugh
at violence when the execution
is poor; stop laughing when it interrupts
curves we recognize as a face,
or another piece of anatomy
we can't pretend. But when
an organ reacts by presenting
a new type of spine, a pleat
in the material, we call it
extravagant, since it is personal
and possibly private. When the sanctuary
function we have designated
as a society is destroyed, there is
only the averting of eyes, commentary
shunted beneath our breath, the salt
rubbed into soil not to stop the bleeding
but to accelerate the wrath; to freeze out
an empire of hard truths, a knot where
there should have been suppleness.
Like an index finger, pointing out
clay figures to successor idols as we
struggle to account for a shift in principles
borne by the mire of fatal arguments.

How My Aunt's Abortion Was Like a Fern

We came to know so much
through ferns, those planted
by my father, and those prehistoric:
thousands of years of pressure
and death, compacted until
they became shades
or a reliquary of light,
color suckling on a
declaration of drought,
the charcoal portraits
.
of my aunt who taught us
which shapes are most desirous:
heart for the face, almond for eyes,
thick width of the mouth,
high cheek bones and
lifelong neck; they tried
measuring it once, at a party,
to see if it was as lithe
as the actress's.

We learned how the human
fetal position has been mimicked
by ferns, as if they were
also made in the appropriate
image; how the seemingly
impossible, a soft
nautilus, had to be
nursed throughout
a long day
of waiting for show
and tell in first
or second grade
so I could demonstrate
the self-protective instinct

also applied to plants, as
we were certain it did
in animals. I kept the fern
between wet paper towels,
the likely sum total
of what my aunt
was given to deal with
the caveats that didn't
come on the package
but should have been
understood, given
the unhygienic
conditions.

After school, my mother had me
toss the fern into the ash can,
as she called it, from when
the family garbage was
burned in public; because
you can never unlearn what
nature teaches. You can
only own up to its
terminal existence.

How My Aunt's Abortion Was Like an Alligator Purse

Once upon a time, I wrote a fable,
something Boris Karloff might
have performed in a novelty act,
then recorded on a plastic disc
to be purchased at a swamp meet
by some esoteric hipster, although
at the time it was deadly serious.
My teachers didn't think I was
smart enough for the assignment,
my quotient so low, my voice
undisciplined. I should have
been trained solely as a typist,
I was so fast with text and stream
of consciousness if not sub-
and con-, to wit: I can no longer
tell you exactly how the story went:
alligator, purse, tissue stuffed
in the mouth; my mother loved it
and was puzzled, since she did
not call them purses, but pocketbooks.
It was the east coast way
of knowing your possessions.
My aunt took the story and used it
for her college English class.
She couldn't think of one on her own
though she had lived with sacrifice,
bait and switch, the hunter and hunted,
yet was unable to draw any lesson
from her atonement.

A Model Penitent

In her convalescence, my aunt
became a model: of hands and feet
though nothing of the ruins between.
For nail polish and beauty salons,
footwear and jewelry, all the fashion
disdained by our mother, hard
working as she was, in ammonia
and cleanser up to her knees.
That was the thing with us:

We had no empathy. Not even for
Audrey Hepburn, when she posed
with her neck fully extended in a
magazine we separated from its staples
to get a better grip on the centerfold,
hold it up to the light. It must be
the angle, we decided, or some other
photographer's gimmick; someone
wanted to get a ruler and measure

this travesty, while our mother muttered
something about Tennessee Williams
when Georg Bernard Shaw might have
been more appropriate. Our mother
loved books, and playwrights, and her feet
were flat, blistered, frequently injured
at the ankles. They appeared held together

by wattle and daub, grout running
through her arteries; and my aunt's
were white and rosy, nubile loaves
pulled from the ovens of a holy order.
My sister and I wore corrective shoes
for pigeon toes and fallen arches,
any number of defects that had yet

to be identified but would surely
follow us into adulthood.

There is a Yiddish expression this reminds me of,
one the adults used when telling us to leave
our harassed and exhausted mother alone,
something about the frailty of enamel or
ceramic. Our father often tried it with my aunt
as she took to looking at herself only in parts,
blotting out mistakes with powder, in the mirror
of her compact: in the middle of the eyebrows,
on her chin, a spot on her cheek that insisted
on multiplying all available shine as though
it were a laser, waiting to bore through
to her teeth, and claim the rest of her skeleton.

Previous page: circa 1940
Above: Junior High School, circa 1952

The God(s) That Failed

In the late teens of the 21st century, studies showed that children who grew up around books had better life outcomes. They were better readers, more proficient at math, and more likely to gain employment working in technology. There was no minimum number of books they should have read, but a home library of between eighty and three-hundred books was said to be the most influential on children through adolescence. Above three-hundred books, the returns diminished.

I don't know how many books my parents had in our house. They kept their books in the hall lining the bedrooms. The bookcases, built to my mother's specifications, extended from the floor to the dropped ceiling. The top shelves, which my sister and I could not reach, held the hardbacks: complete sets of Fitzgerald, Faulkner, O'Neil's plays, Bertram Russell, Hume, Will and Ariel Durant, and Edward Gibbon. On the bottom shelves, secured behind a cabinet, were the paperbacks, stuffed in every which way and always on the verge of an avalanche: *Escape from Freedom. Walden II. Childhood and Society. The Autobiography of Malcolm X. How to Talk Dirty and Influence People. Darkness at Noon.*

And *The God That Failed. The God That Failed* is a reassessment of Communism by writers, artists, and politicians who had declared themselves apostates. The book's introduction acknowledges how difficult it was, even for fellow travelers, to renounce their faith and membership in the Party. For many, it had come to be their identity, a lens for looking at a world in turmoil, introducing themselves into it, and judging others.

People became Communists, the introduction says, out of "despair and loneliness;" because of the dearth of choices for those opposed to fascism, but also disappointed in liberalism and western democracy. Renouncing Communism created a "terrible conflict of conscience" for those who had stocked such faith in it, because there were so few options for their activism. Leaving the Party was agonizing for some, the introduction says, and sometimes deadly for others.

My parents were neither sympathizers nor fellow travelers. You might call them Communist Curious, or a Cold War couple. My father had his own brushes with the allure and stain of Communism. He was teaching junior high in an isolated desert community when, during the height of the Rosenberg spy case, he was denied tenure. His name was Rosenberg, after all, and each weekend, he took mysterious trips to the big bad city of Los Angeles (where he was studying for his master's, and his parents lived). My mother's contacts were even more fleeting: she purchased Mao's Little Red Book when it was published in the U.S. (and coincidentally sold on the steps of her alma mater by the Black Panthers). When I swiped the book for my own collection while I was in college, she complained I was stealing her property without acknowledging the irony. She also voted for Dorothy Healey, the so-called "Red Queen of Los Angeles," for county assessor in 1966. As a poll worker, she counted two votes for Healey in her precinct; one was her own and the other would turn out to be her father's.

As tenuous, or as spurious, as their own relationship to Communism was, the ideology fueled the debates that would become the seminal rhetorical conflicts of their age. My parents especially made an obsession of the Hollywood Ten, and they worshipped Dashiell Hammett and Lillian Hellman. Hammett's mysteries, Hellman's many memoirs and the biographies written of them as individuals and as a couple were among the volumes my parents claimed equal custody of in the hallway bookcases. There were also innumerable books about the Rosenbergs, the Pumpkin Papers, Whittaker Chambers, and Alger Hiss. Like Fitzgerald, Faulkner, O'Neil, and others, the Communist martyrs of the 1950s stood as my parents' equivalents of stadium rock stars, or today's tabloid or social media celebrities. The longer any one of these figures had been dead, the more my parents rehashed the gossip about them, reliving spats and scandals that many of their peers must have forgotten, if they had ever been interested. These were the gods my parents focused on, though they were not like the God they had my sister and I study at Hebrew school. These were Greek and Roman deities, subject to the same insecurities and appetites that bedevil humans. They would torment my parents too.

There were other gods, of course: CBS News correspondents, the professors they remembered from their college years; adults who became known to me and my sister because they played a pivotal role in our lives beyond the public school classroom. Hy Rothman might have been one. He was a longtime friend of my paternal grandfather. Tall, distant, uninterested in me and my sister, and in children in general, he was a contractor who specialized in down market apartments. But he also built the house I grew up in. He had taken on the project of my parents' house on a dare; he wanted to prove he could create something just as nice as any prestigious, brand name outfit could. He was to become a standout example of manly, American success in the world as my parents would have had me see it. He was a capitalist, or at least the product of a mixed economy that subsidized some at the expense of others. But there were no books written by or about him. It was possible he was not even a reader.

Such was the inconsistent, unbalanced pantheon that our parents built for us; the bookcase was where we paid homage when my sister and I had nothing better to do, because all the neighborhood kids were busy, or didn't want to play with us. We played with the books, taking them off the shelves, testing our mother's patience. We did not read the books, since their subject matter seemed so adult, or obtuse; and their lengths seemingly endless. But we did open up the table of contents and the dedication pages. We took turns looking through them, and wondering what it was you had to do, to get a book dedicated to yourself. Then we'd try re-arranging the books into towers, sometimes fortresses. Eventually we'd have to restore the books back to their natural environments, while our mother tried not to let on how much stress this caused, watching her children navigate through stacks so precariously balanced.

While we were in junior high and high school, my sister and I were able to occasionally consult some of our parents' books for research projects. We were also encouraged by one particular junior high school teacher to explore our parents' libraries to meet the semester's reading quota. I specifically remember pulling out a copy of *The Good Earth,* which I thought would impress this teacher but didn't. My father introduced me to W. Somerset Maugham through his reserves, and I found Jacqueline Susann, Harold Robbins, and Irving Wallace tomes to entertain me when I was desperate. In 1981, while I was at college and my sister was about to graduate high school, our parents divorced. My mother became increasingly outspoken against religion afterward, but that is probably another story. She kept the house; my father moved out. His books--college textbooks, the real estate manuals, the volumes of practice exams, political tomes, the works of popular psychology and pedagogy—stayed behind. My mother began to add to them at a furious pace.

Liberated by the divorce to indulge her interests, my mother became a collector of relics from her childhood: toys, machines, dishes, board games, models, train sets. But she was most adept at finding books. She specialized in the work of playwright Thorton Wilder. He was the son of missionaries, which my mother could understand, since she was an Army brat, and was similarly traipsed around the world by her parents. Always fascinated by F. Scott and Zelda Fitzgerald, she pursued a hard cover edition of Budd Schulberg's *The Disenchanted,* for decades. (The book is supposedly based on an incident in F. Scott Fitzgerald's life.) She was a more than casual fan of Norman Mailer (she had always been impressed with his depiction of war in *The Naked and the Dead*) and bought all the Mailer she could find. Her most enduring passion was for Robert Penn Warren's *All the King's Men*, which ignited an obsession with Huey Long. She devoured biographies and self-published obscurities about Long in search of an explanation for his rise and fall by assassination.

The books my mother compiled spilled out of the bookcase, into her bedroom, my former bedroom, and eventually the kitchen. My father, meanwhile, could not read for years after the split. He lost the ability to concentrate, or to be distracted. He had always been a nervous type, troubled about his abilities and intellect. This may have stemmed from his genes, or his upbringing, or some combination that remained unfathomable to him up until his death. He learned to find pleasure in reading again many years later but lost the ability to comprehend text after a stroke in 2011. The only thing he read then, I believe, were billboards, as I drove him around town when I visited.

The house had to be sold after my mother and sister died within nine months of each other, between 2009 and 2010. I had to go through the books again. I felt as though I was parceling out my parents' minds, particularly my mother's, as I sorted and re-sorted the books into piles. I found pocketbook versions of James Baldwin's earliest works, and Eldridge Cleaver's *Soul on Ice,* which must have driven my father around the bend; he was known to snap at racist bait when it was offered. I kept my mother's copy of Schulberg's *The Disenchanted*, because I remembered all of the effort she put into finding it. Her first editions of Wilder, along with Long's manifesto, *Every Man a King,* went to her alma mater's library. I also unearthed a cache of movie tie-ins of Kevin Costner films, which she must have justified to herself as satisfying her curiosity about Wyatt Earp and other Old West figures who became technical consultants to the Hollywood films that mythologized them. I think, however, she just liked to look at Costner. All of those, along with so many others, went to the thrift store where she had volunteered.

That was when I discovered *The God That Failed*, a paperback of yellowed pages I had never recalled seeing as a child. But I knew immediately what it was, and what it must have meant to my parents. I understood that the book, like so many others there, represented my parents' shared history: how they met and why they may have been attracted and eventually repulsed by each other. These books were the physical embodiment of their compulsions and convictions, what they hoped to provide to us in the form of an education; what they thought we needed to get through this life, or at least living an examined one.

My parents were lonely people, before their marriage and after their divorce, although my mother coped with it much more easily than my father. There are as many explanations for this as there are books my parents read; and possibly even more explanations for how my sister's life turned out. She earned a lot of money, but never moved out of that house. She may have had a girlfriend in high school, but after that, there was no other romantic relationship. My own life has been fine, though I had a troubled start. I have spent probably too much time trying to figure out why my family was so shattered by the events of its time. I am the only one left of a life that seemed to revolve around that house, and its books. The exigencies of time (the closing of the sale on the house) and space (my New York apartment) forced me to give up all those books, and I regretted it. I regret it still.

I regret it each time I think of my sister and I playing beside the bookcase, delightfully unaware of all that was unfolding around us. We built monuments composed of words and ideas that enchanted those strange creatures who dominated us: our parents. We were taught not just to simply honor our father and mother, but to admire their educations, their engagement with the present, their comprehension of the past. There seemed to be nothing they did not or could not know, until they were presented with a scenario for which no book could prepare them.

The God(s) That Failed

1.

In the world of our fathers,
the name is a fetish:
El jefe, der Chef, the head
of the table for Sunday dinners
because that was how it was
done in the military, rather
than by the religious method.
Drop the original for a rank,
a feminine for initials:
as in the degrees everyone
wanted for my sister academically;
for me, they wanted nothing.
Hence, the generic.
The greatest source of tension
amid the pebbles at the bottom
of the goldfish bowl that was
my parents' marriage
had to do with who was looking in
at any moment, whether they
were kibitzers at this American thing
or whether all that had been absorbed
by charcoal and cotton meant
to keep the aquarium sparkling.
My aunt made it so she sounded
richer than she was, before the machinery
of echoes proved her womb to be transparent.
Or maybe it was invisible, permanently,
ending the suspense
and the register
of the dead,
or creating what was altogether new,
another scarlet letter.

2.

At the end of her life, my mother
had to recite all of the names
from her family before she could
get to mine, which had become
a strange appellation.
I had to wait for all of the aunts
she grew up with,
the uncles they married,
the brother she was so lonesome for
but never her mother, even though
she was never "Mom" or "Mommy"
or "Mother," but like Warhol's superstars
answered exclusively to a succinct,
definitive nickname.
Only my uncle employed the word
"Mother" on the intercom system
that bound together the thousands
of square feet he purchased to secure
his parents in, at the dawn of the space age.
His handwriting was resolutely atrocious in that way
the best doctors insist on maintaining,
so he typed it up: "Mother's Room,"
and taped the paper beside the button
corresponding to my grandparents.
This is how I learned about family relations.
I still remember the spew and shadow
that the portable typewriter ink and keys made,
honing letters as though they meant for a metal
plaque, their significance not to be confused
for crumbs or tea leaves,
the shapes that reveal the future
in wells of saucers and the dregs of cups.

Weeds

After "Nets," Jen Bervin

Weeds newly made
plentiful and clamoring
about the corner of cement
collapsing into pre-soils,
pebbles sacked by weathering,
as sections of sidewalk pull
and twist away as if in
a spasm of resistance:
because where else
could this kind of growth
find comfort and aid
for such a liminal existence.
Perhaps where crossing
the channel by boat is
impossible, and sky is the last
alternative; or where my father
and his father tried to clear
a path among sanctioned
real estate captains but failed
in their demands, foreclosures,
bankruptcies, and ruined
commitments. They were unable
to attract the right pilgrims
to do the hard work for them:
the hands-and-knees,
switchblade and thumb,
the extraction in timing
and excuses. Come on, everyone.
Haven't you ever flopped
in public? Or were you too proud,
chauvinistic in promenading
along like the thistle and mustards,
bitter but in a rough peace over
when to strike, how deep to burrow,

because shade eventually comes
on every clock, and blame
is another kind of blossom.

Circa early 1940s

Cypress Bells

The cypress, at rest,
hums when the wind
is ready to count its fragments:
salt, mist, larval thoughts
of wives about who will make
the swifter claim to
happiness in the afterlife;
whether they will live to witness
the middle ages of their children
or if they'll have to speculate
based on report cards
and candid photographs.
Once everyone is free from
the rules of this civilization
they will make their own
for others, and those rules
will play like the rhythm
the cypress makes: fingers
worrying the rim of wine glasses,
the kind my mother used
to serve the cheap stuff,
piss sweet with a German label
most familiar to her brother and parents.
In proper amounts, it could pack
a real sucker punch, though they
rarely got there; they were satisfied
by the simple access to taste,
if not the apex. Or perhaps they
delighted there was one thing that
schmo they had her marry, couldn't
take away from them, since he was
under doctor's orders not to use
his most treasured sense, or calculate
the pressure or direction of air as
it rousts tethered chimes into sound,

based on what the sun tosses into
deeper space, the time it takes to hit
the earth, and the outer reaches
of one particular consciousness.

1967 or Approximate

On the way home from immaculate
Canada, my parents stopped a drunk
woman from getting into her car in
Seattle. In Oregon my sister tested
her water pistols in the brackish
falls, but what use were they,
when they could not get us seats in
any of the restaurants. Down into
the Central Valley where my father
cultivated business contacts, landless
farmers and asparagus planters,
the same particulate matter between
their teeth that someone had tried
to swindle from their fathers. Our
father at the wheel, trying not to
buzz on mirages, our mother speaking
in her most calibrated tone, translating
everyone's eroding pronunciations
to weave through our father's deafness.
My wash and wear grandmother in her
shrunken dress, because no one
else would sit next to me with my
habit of car sickness. We pulled into
the city limits and on the last curve
before our house, our father slowed
to take in the view, as if it were a
Christmas scene or a lighted abacus. Our
neighbors huddled on the cliff road
as a helicopter searchlight scoured
the ravine for something to
salvage, and we learned a pair of cars
had just sailed into the twilight ahead,
a drag race gone wrong, a couple
of boys, into the bands of broken fever
we'd been fleeing, ruddy and rust-bound,

a crush of mauve and purpled blood;
not real colors but catalysts that had
stolen our air and tomorrow would
replace it with smog. We begged our father
not to stop, not to brag to the neighbors
about how far we'd come, and how
fast, but it was his last moment of
command in the family, and a chance
to take in all that he had accomplished.

Likely Vancouver, British Columbia, circa early 1950s

Scenes From My Parents' Marriage

I've seen where the revoluntionaries stood,
unmarked but for a dent in the sidewalk,
a dropped head, a high heel inserted
into the peace of wet concrete setting.
The sun must have been glorious that minute,
splashing against the gray plaza as if remaking
time itself, against the cobbled walks and
classical buildings, a repository of someone
else's troubles resolved through pressed shoulders
and wild applause, rending what my mother called
the veil of civilization. That was all which separated
her from a layer of death she saw herself walking
in, as though she saw herself in a canyon of wax
figures flapping nonsense from their mouths
to oil their gums, her jaw stiff, uncoupled,
unable to put a voice to the things she knew,
where she had been. My father might say she
choked on her own reason. He took in everything
he knew in the abstract, words without breath;
he sacrificed his hopes to his wife's convalescence.
This is how his world ended, in astringent sentences
of hangnails, bad grades, his daughter's dirty faces.
No one cares where these terrors took root, how they
divided friends and family on a terrace though all
had an equal view to the scaffolding.

The Set Dresser

My father loved the movies:
In high school he entered a contest
to win a date with Elizabeth Taylor.
Imagine the minds I would have
unlocked had I been gifted with
her violet-fire eyes, the calibration
of her nose, mouth, and eyebrows;
the timbre of her speech;
as though I had been finely wrought
and polished, a bell as clear as the sky
used to be, the way my mother talked
about it as she lit a cigarette, tapped
the ash on to the patio, and swept it
into the garden plot with the bottoms
of her feet.

The After Plants

Like weeds, the bougainvillea
are wanton, as our father found
the dandelions that demoralized
his gardening; their seeds dispersing
like salt tossed over the shoulder, or
something from which you might wrest
a serum. There are only two ways
to think about time once the divorce
is final: the facts as established on paper
and those of the ether. My mother
always hated the cypress installed
by the neighboring future divorcee
but held her tongue until after
my father left; with the after plants,
purple and rusted red, she found it
possible to assert her own perimeter.
On trellises they confronted
their own view to the canyon,
beyond the cypress's webbed panes,
like hook and ladder systems
that entangle fish, wrangling them
into martyrdom: what every divorced man
considers to be his fate in the dreams
of his release, yet finds them in daylight
to be his own singular vision.

Reception

The center of a sunflower is a parabolic curve.
I didn't copy this from some textbook,
but figured it out by looking at satellite dishes.
They crop up in Queens, the dishes do,
the outer borough equivalent of kudzu,
relegated to terraces and roofs of second
floor apartments meant to have a feel of
a real house, standing alone and proud,
a socially acceptable marking of territory.
I'm sorry. I hadn't meant this to be so angry.
I hadn't intended this to have so much form
or substance; only as an observation as to how
data is collected, stored for purposes of reproducing
stunning replicas. There are only so many shapes
in nature and everything else is Ecclesiastes;
a perfect circle comes with nary a deviation
from the original spectacle. My father's
hearing aids followed the shape of wasps' bellies,
heavy with wood, or the venom pumped into
arbitrary victims, the receiver species with
three fine bones and a gathering of hair,
lambent with sound, and shivering.

My Father Attempts to Explain Billie Holiday to Us

People are born with habits,
cigarettes, alcohol, spitting
the moistened ends of spent cigars
into the flower beds—an indulgence
taken up by my father and grandfather,
because everyone knows that ash
and plant matter are beneficial
to roses and snapdragons. At bottom,
a belief, as when my father said
as a young teacher he was convinced
anyone could be made to excel provided
he had the right environment: chance
and rhythm. More deterministic
drivel, as what might emerge through
a sieve of blood and proteins, or
the discussions we had, going around
the dinner table. Just where did
my sister's red hair come from, my
own dirty blonde; my father's ulcer
and asthma, my mother's rotting
teeth and gums; the exhaust of her
Marlboros, ascending to the ceiling,
as if heeding a call for the next
passage out, a promise that will turn
shadows to sand, silk to windows,
bread for a break on stage, to tremble
in a dress that is a revelation of muscle.
I was always left wondering,
at the evening's conclusion, whether
my father would have traded the sound
of his voice for the bracing peril
of experience before he went deaf,
and then tasked himself with settling
into the temptation of a vacuum.

My Father, the Deaf Man, Describing Billie Holiday's Voice

He had to use his hands
for emphasis on the dots
and dashes, or some other
cypher of sight and dimension,
the clear-as-a-bell quality
we used to assign to the sky
after rain, the high season
of spasms and swelling in
his chest, because he was
first an asthmatic before
the shipwreck of his auditory
senses. Not much could
outrun the buzz and background
that roared through his
hearing: the stall and rattle
of his struggling breath;
air that circulated through
smoke and brass, the sweet
and acrid path it took into
his remaining perceptions;
the relief of cool skin
from stone fruit against
his lips when one of his
requisite fevers lodged
into his forehead.
A recollection that had
to be tended as though
one of those eternal candles
in the synagogue, or filaments
of tungsten over the names
of the dead. "Tart" was finally
the word he came up with,
something prohibited and
betraying that the throat

is afraid to swallow, the teeth
on edge as it melts at the roof
of the mouth, a sin digested
long before the taste exits
the last of the sensory organs,
buried somewhere beyond
where they could be adjusted.

Another World to Come

Within my pillar of salt
called Los Angeles, I naturally
think of my parents, lost to
the elements: air, soil, sea,
as per their strict instructions,
preventing their reactants
from becoming products,
virulent gases or blips
and glitches of minerals
from across the continents,
deciding how the day
will go. The spread of red
tissue across the horizon:
salt refusing its bonds
with sand in the desert;
twinges of sepia between
echelons of healing
and stasis: exhaust from
rifts in the planet. The price
of sugar and pigs and the food
between them may triple,
to say nothing of the cost
of lung transplants. My father,
deaf and bullied by allergens
so minute they had yet to be
named, categorized, isolated,
huffed on his inhaler every year
during Days of Awe, the most solemn
in a disregarded practice.
My mother summoned the shine
of anthracite onto slate
steps with each swipe of
her waterlogged paintbrush.
Together, they used to toast
the sunset with smoke on

the patio they loved, his cigar
and her cigarette adding
wheals and streaks to the grooves
of the twilight, comparing
notes on how they prepped
the children that day for
the coming societal collapse.
All that particulate matter
made for such diverting
confines separating daylight
from dusk, and dusk from eventide,
anything to chase away the demands
of their shared remaining senses,
or, to be most prescient,
just one: the art
of contact.

My Parents' Divorce

What I want to know, most of all,
is whether the tree feels the phantom
of a butchered limb; does the phloem
stiffen where the branch fails to
carry its share of the sky; how much
of an ache might spiral through
surviving xylem? There are so many
questions, to be truthful, though like
discussing the values of someone's
marriage, we can answer only with
assumptions. Did the dried soil cry
out as my mother uprooted elephant
ears and ferns? Or was it relieved
when presented with a new and unfamiliar
burden: the roses she had coveted
through years of a rain forest adjacent
landscape, sheltering my father's ambitions
to own a piece of the miracle in the desert.
Certainly the roses made fewer demands
than the fruitless process my father planted
as the whitewash on stucco was shocking
in its reflection, brazen in its statement
about who had purchased the house,
what he believed, when was he willing
to risk his life, sacrifice those of his wife
and children. The second thing my mother
did while taking over the quarter-acre was
to paint the blue trim green, a color to recall
how the first temple was built, with foreign
materials that could not complain as they
were pulled from the mountains and transported
to a new life of service, and priestly silence.

Imperceptible

After "Disappearing Queen," Gail Martin

To disappear, you need first to have been visible:
Noticed, indelible, constant as the light made
As collateral; as a byproduct of legs, wings,
The transfer of pollens; to be burned some day
For a quarter, a dollar, a remembrance
That forestalls a loss until the mourners
Are called back from their sorrows
Into their chores, their customs,
The formalities of getting through
To the next day, and days afterward.

For the rest of us, thin, sour, flowerless
And without a flicker, there is no way
To escape what we could not have been;
In ink, paper, wax or parchment; a picture
That did not arise in the batch of silver
Nitrate; or a taste our weak jaws failed
To sink into, beyond the marrow of an
Erased animal. Yet we live on, last,
Best and unbreakable, the wick secured
In the middle of the candle, or debris
Scraping the bottom of a square bottle,
Wilted spices and granular minerals
Chosen for irrelevance by chance,
Some decision to reach for the other vial.

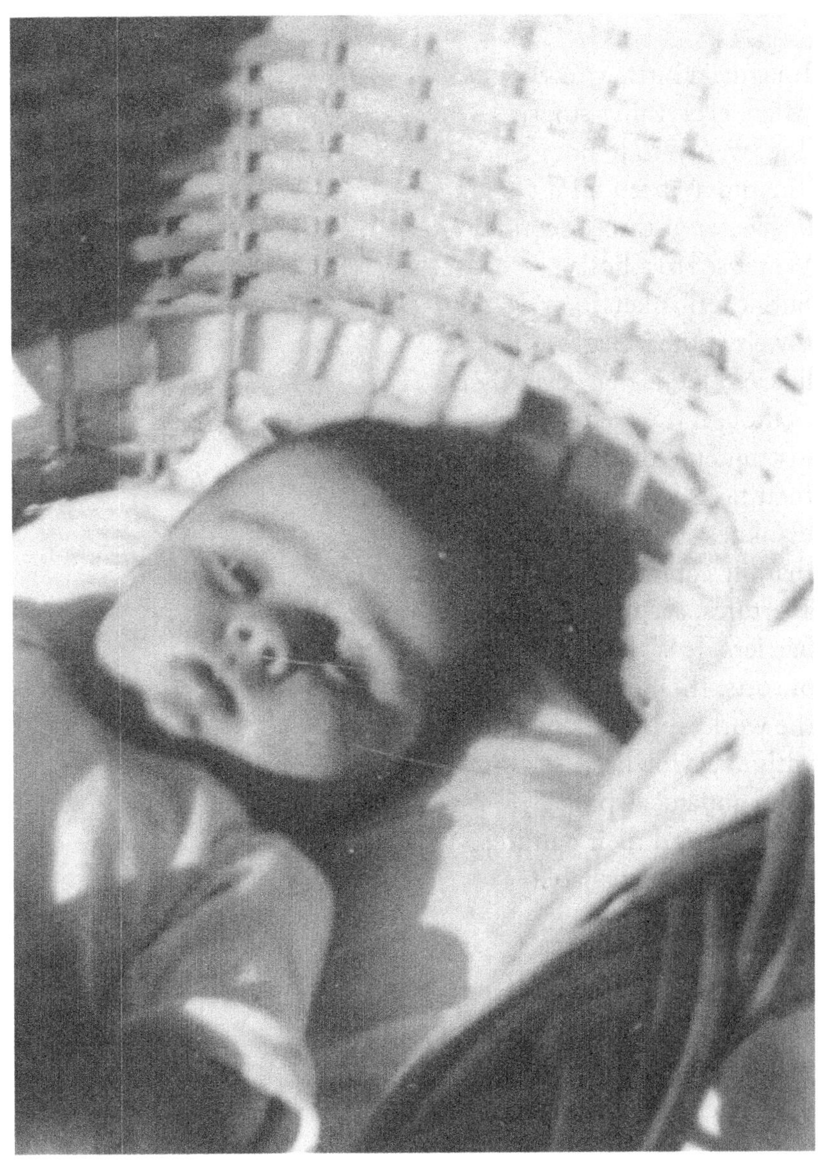

1939

Stillbirth

Imagine a birth
where everything stops.
The twenty-four-hour clock.
The timer at ten minutes
or five, or at three seconds.
Water set to a boil.
Surgical blankets,
towels and bandages,
lips and teeth that sever tissue
as though it were fabric,
instruments that have inherited
their tasks by virtue of their spiritual
blankness. Threads and needles
that ply cataracts, repair
apertures, secure
barriers. It is still a birth
of sorts, though
the world spins
with new violence;
palm and eucalyptus
lurch beyond their cultures,
roots indistinguishable
from branches.
Years from now,
who will remain curious
enough to count these interior layers;
whether they are a compilation
of worries or seasons, or a story
of rats hanging on for dear life
beneath the fronds as the wind
took what it could, without
breath or breeze, throughout a force
equal to an earthquake.

The Remains

The skin a slip
of what a child might lose
on a bicycle, the skid
against asphalt,
rendering a joint
suddenly fruit and liquid,
in need of a gauze support
if it is to harden properly.
I can't say why I've always
imagined the assemblage
being placed in an envelope,
exquisitely folded paper
given a sudden new responsibility.
To be sent to a locker
at the bus station, as if
a lock of hair, a scent crushed
between the pages of a book,
a plot no one cares to remember,
then retrieved to make a point
rendered moot. Outside it might
be like foil sundered from
wax paper wrappers, how girls
entertained one another
after lunch period, torturing
packages, comparing the dexterity
of their fingers, their stubby
nails with no effect on
the thick, almost acid
feeling to their cuticles,
the peel of citrus.

The Lost

We had a habit of losing
people in my family, as if
they were socks in the laundry
my mother tortured. She boiled
our clothes, she said, since we
were so filthy, my sister and I;
to say nothing of how she rendered
anything in pairs irreconcilable,
stained by brighter items, stretched
if not exiled. Like my grandfather's
stepfather, or the brother we heard
about but could never find.
The women who made *aliyah*
before there was an Israel, off
the grid until their great-grandchildren
began flying missions over Lebanon.
They said for a couple of kibbutzniks
life in the military was not that bad,
the equivalent of the American myth
of upward mobility: the sky's the limit.

Before my mother's illness—before
the abortion that was supposed to be
an adoption, the sibling I might still
have or the cousin—there were the books
and movies my parents shared, ideas
about moral obligation, what to do
with troubled friends and relatives.
There was one TV show they particularly
loved, but like the woman my mother
used to be, there's no record of
that show, though it's thought
today to have been very influential.
In that same period doctors had
yet to fabricate a sound for those

we know to be silent, until screams
were put to the mouths of those
meant to be saved whether they
were souls or not, or spikes in a
continuum of unrealized intellects.

After the Abortion: Construction

The summer after my aunt's
abortion, I learned to play "War."
Knowing which cards were
greater than or less than was
about all the math I could
handle as the new high-rise
rose above our ears. My grandmother
availed herself of extra creams
and powders, polished surfaces,
scrubbed floors, anything to cut
the dust pouring in from our soon-to-be
neighbors in progress. After our
card games, I'd build card houses
on the glass coffee table, careful
not to scratch it like gravel or
pebbles could. The mud pumped
out from the job site made a levy
we had to climb over, to get to the market.
We bought flour and baking powder,
sometimes white sugar like the new
building's mortar. Its bricks were a
buffed off-color, like the underside
of human tissue rubbed raw
as if someone was searching
for a virgin organ. My aunt,
recovering, tried a similar tint
on her lips and nails; like the bumpy
matting beneath the carpet.
It showed itself sometimes when
we vacuumed, suction against
the fibers and plywood,
just another secret, like me
in the adults-only building,
to be kept from the landlord.

After the Abortion: The Cuttings

My landless grandfather
sold produce for a living;
my grandmother grew avocados.
A hydroponic orchard on
the window sills in jelly jars,
from pits she saved from
making salads. As her daughter
languished between complications
from a contaminated
procedure, she cultivated
a cascade of creeping
charlottes and charlies,
Wandering Jews and spider
plants, species that could
easily prosper in a dark apartment.

Low maintenance, no brainers:
That's how we'd characterize
them today but we lacked
the words then; there were
either green thumbs or black
ones; we know which side
of the family I favored.
The plants swayed above us
in the macramćd harnesses
my mother was taught
to make during her mental
convalescence, along with
ceramic ashtrays, tile mosaics,
and moccasins with no
support for fragile arches,
so my sister and I could not
wear them. My grandmother
watered the plants, dusted
their leaves, talked to them

as I waited for avocado pits
to split open like the earth's
core would once the world
ended. Or at least when
California broke off into
the ocean, which was
forecasted to occur
at just about any minute.
My grandmother eventually
transplanted stems and new
roots she had single-handedly
germinated into potted soil,
but they never bore fruit,
nor climbed above my knees.
Yet they were the only
anchored creatures in
the one-and-a-half bedroom unit,
if you didn't count the white
rocks in a brass cauldron,
supporting the plastic palm tree.

Pulmonary Therapy

Punished in the lungs,
in conversions and pulses,
as though this was no mere sentence,
but a stab at rehabilitation
made permanent, therapeutics
of the terminal. Mount the board,
hang by the ankles, beat
the congestion out of
the cavities; an emptying
improbable and coercive.
It might look advanced
or contemporary, the equivalent
of pounding the dust from
an oriental carpet on the balcony
of a foreign embassy I might
witness years from then,
and pine for now. Or it might
resemble an exercise that clears
the mind, realigns the vertebrae,
to reclaim a birthright, before
the flames licked at the muzzle
of otherwise gentle animals,
nudging pasture and grasses
into a kinder stage
of wreckage.

Largess

My father lived off the largess
of bud, branch, and breath that reached
into the firmament, where it might
have been better welcomed
than on the lips he tried to read
to compensate for his deafness.
On his own he sought the cinnamon
he said would ease his diabetes;
as a child he chewed on sticks
like some tough guy with a cigar,
a stevedore or a gangster; as an adult,
he sprinkled it in his tea, though
it had no effect on his vitals.
If the pressure pricked high,
his sugar drilled low, and vice
versa; he sumptuously kept
a record of every blip, gasp,
and hiccup of his functions
and fortune, what made him
rich in the abstract, or doomed
for the inevitable wet blanket
that extinguished net and gross.
He often made a great exhibit
of his yellow legal pads but it was
the underside of the paper that
was more informative, a vascular map
wrought by the force he applied
the pen to paper, as if he meant
to carve an apology to my mother,
a rare act of remorse. She was
the accountant in the family, said
she'd show him how to cheat
on the taxes so he could better
keep his half but he refused
because he was committed

to failure, as a scholar depends
on the footnotes. At the bottom
of each page, he left the date,
time, and his signature, as if he had
created a work of art, a portrait
of all his achievements and what
nourished him, out of someone
else's deficits.

Time is Relative

When I asked my mother how
old I was as our family began
to crack and peel, she said only,
"You and your sister were just
children," which might have
meant before we tried painting
a mural on the side of the house
with doves and peace symbols;
definitely before my father made
us wash it off, the cleanser bleaching
a shadow onto the walls as if the stucco
were haunted; or before I let the boy
next door throw my orthopedic
shoes into the ivy though how
could I have stopped him; he
was so much taller than all
of us, parents included; or maybe
it was before my mother's father
had his first heart attack although
there would be two others, on top
of his Parkinson's.

I wonder if my daughter was
ever that same age or if her time
would be seamless, unmarked
but for benign occasions, the fight
we had at her gymnastics class
about taking her stuff off the table
after I had lugged up four long
blocks and the staircase; or when
she was frightened by my yelling
at my father over long distance
after he called the Fire Department
but refused to get into the ambulance.
He was having second thoughts

about the hospital, the paramedics.
Perhaps the firefighters recognized
him as the man who once left
his oven on, smoking out
the entire building. This was,
after all, only his first stroke,
or the first one anyone noticed.
There would be others, smaller
episodes, we would lose track of
until the last one which left him
broken and restless.

From the Gutter

Everyone's dead now, so why don't I
spill it: in high school my boyfriend
got some other girl pregnant. I wasn't
as surprised as I was upset, picturing
the inciting act like meat marinating
in something fake, maybe liquid smoke,
or having griller lines painted on it
for a menu, to suggest the rustic.
Her teeth were huge, crooked, and
haunted, by her lip gloss, maybe milk,
as if they were pieces of dry ice, lifted
from their fog, the corporeal equivalent of
moth balls, fuming at the back of
a forbidden closet. We'd go in there
when we were kids, my sister and I,
at our grandmother's, to run our hands
through her minks and leopards.
They were at least as satisfying as
the plunge our feet took into the gutter
as we walked home, having forgot
our sandals. Our toes had to curl to
a certain degree, against the slimy
bottom, so we wouldn't slip and have
to breathe in the concrete. I imagined
her toes had to do the same, atop a
bare mattress or the stirrups' sanitary
plastic coverlets. You don't ever want
any limb to grow cold, any appendage.
Because then you can't run away,
when you were caught walking through
the gray water, and your father is
handing down the punishments.

After the Abortion III

Once it was all over,
the debates and obligations,
duties fulfilled, and children
spared from the shame,
my grandmother forsook
her dream of living by the water
and moved east, closer to us grandkids.
On the way to her new place,
there was a landmark restaurant.
You entered through the mouth of
a whale-sized fish into a crimson maw
of overstuffed furniture. I always wanted
to go inside but my parents said no,
I wouldn't like it. My grandmother
promised she'd never live
so far away again, although
the new apartment shared with
the former the same two-mile radius
centered around a space age gas station.

My mother divorced my father.
She took up hobbies, old obsessions,
what my father couldn't tolerate
because it was disorganized, frivolous:
clutter like her parents had collected.
She filled what had been my bedroom
with model trains, board games, doll houses,
books and cash registers, adding machines,
erector sets, cast metal cars, miniature airplanes.
In the hall closet she compiled
a collection of vacuum cleaners.
She had her best friend photograph her
vacuuming the desert, that first weekend

they went away without their husbands,
because some dust
never settles.

Tickle

My feet were up on the headrest
of the car's front seat, a position
reminiscent of an experience I
hadn't had yet; but one my aunt
must have been familiar with,
as all women are if they are to be
fitted or inspected, so they don't
fly off the handle, or plunge into

barrenness, like a plot of barely laid
asphalt for a temporary parking lot,
where my grandmother went next
door for her groceries. Right near
a pair of uncanny gas station signs
that a volatile movie star had
photographed and called his
composition "Double Standard."
Critics thought it reflected only
the most obvious aspect of the city's
petroleum soaked history,

though now they look at this picture
and call it quaint or whimsical;
natives might score a few
points by identifying the time
and relevant intersections involved
to make this insight permanent;

or where my aunt raised a finger
to my bare feet, always withholding
actual contact, but the anticipation
had me keening like a banshee.
A tickle or a threat to send me
into convulsions, an episode long
before you were born and might

mistake for torture, though it was
before I was able to forge relationships
on my own, or at least those that
would carry me through life like
a sailboat, or an elevator, or the heat
that rises to undermine the tar
and gravel poured to secure
a safe harbor.

Recovery: circa late 1970s

Hamsa

If you look closely at the creature
from the motion pictures, you'll spot
between costumed fingers and wrist
a human palm: open, vulnerable,
as if to declare a warning or asking
someone to read its lifeline, to see
whether it would end its time as a
mutant or hominid. You latch onto the most
familiar part of any monster encountered
because how else would you know
what to be afraid of? By its asymmetrical
fortunes, it's possible, or the truth told
in its anatomy, what we imagine as ugliness
or opposite though deep down there,
in the murky eddies, there is something
restorative. My aunt came of age in the era
of female behemoths: wasps, she-spiders,
atomic accidents, or the deliberately
outspoken automobiles that spoke
of space travel, orbits on big fins
at a high volume, fueled by ostentatious
opinions. My aunt spent hours arguing
with my father over the first woman
school board candidate, yet within
she kept something small, even inarticulate,
like a squirrel or sparrow our mother told us
never to touch for fear its offspring
would be forever marked. Perhaps
if my aunt had opened her fists as
she asked for help, shown her skin
to be the flawed, natural mechanism
it was, she wouldn't have been labeled
as the freak she is known as, but instead
another child in the grip of the gods.

Jane Rosenberg LaForge is the author of three previous collections of poetry; four chapbooks of poetry; a memoir; and two novels. Her 2018 novel, *The Hawkman: A Fairy Tale of the Great War* (Amberjack Publishing), was a finalist in two categories in the Eric Hoffer awards. Her 2021 novel, *Sisterhood of the Infamous* (New Meridian Arts Press), was a finalist for regional fiction (west) in the National Indie Excellence Awards. She has also been nominated for the Pushcart Prize for poetry and short fiction; and the Best of the Net for poetry.

Made in the USA
Middletown, DE
06 December 2022